Defending Hearth and Home
North Carolina's Revolutionary War Heroines

By Louisa Emmons

Defending Hearth and Home
North Carolina's Revolutionary War Heroines

Hollow Tree Press
P.O. Box 124
Morganton, NC 28680

All inquiries should be addressed to the author through the publisher.

Printed in the United States of America

This book or any portion thereof may not be reproduced or used in any manner whatsoever without the express written permission of the author except for the use of brief quotations in a book review.

Copyright © 2017 Louisa Emmons

All rights reserved.

ISBN-10: 0692632263
ISBN-13: 978-0692632260 (Hollow Tree Press)

About the Author

Louisa Emmons is the author of several award-winning books about North Carolina history. Her first book, *Tales from a Civil War Plantation: Creekside*, won the Robert Bruce Cook Family History Book Award from the North Carolina Society of Historians. Her books *Civil War Voices from Western North Carolina: Letters from the Battlefield and the Home Front* and *Glen Alpine Springs Hotel: A History of Burke County's Finest Accommodation* each won Willie Parker Peace History Book Awards. *Morning Comes to Appalachia*, a collection of poetry chronicling historical events in western North Carolina won a Multimedia Award.

Contents

Preface

The Role of Women in Colonial North Carolina..............1

Penelope Padgett Barker..........................4

Martha McFarlane Bell..........................7

Hannah Millikan Blair..........................10

Rachel Craighead Caldwell..........................12

Sarah Robinson Erwin..........................16

Elizabeth Hutchinson Jackson..........................18

Grace Greenlee McDowell..........................21

Margaret O'Neil McDowell..........................24

Susannah Twitty Miller..........................26

Mary Hooks Slocumb..........................29

Elizabeth Maxwell Steele..........................34

Kerenhappuch Norman Turner..........................37

Bibliography..........................41

Preface

In the course of my research about women of the Revolution, it quickly became apparent that women of that age were defined in large measure by the professions and actions of the males in their families—fathers, husbands and sons. In some cases, I believe these women were recognized for their heroic actions not only because of their actions, but also because they were married to prominent men and, therefore, reports of their heroic behavior became public knowledge more readily. I regret that there were probably many fine, patriotic women of the American Revolution whose exploits may never be known simply because they came from humble beginnings and did not have notable spouses or families to promote or publicize their exemplary acts. Nevertheless, that reality does nothing to detract from the bravery of the daughters of North Carolina that I have selected for this book. It is merely a consequence of the social and cultural climate of that time period.

During the 1700s, North Carolina was in a state of rapid colonization, particularly by the Scots-Irish who emigrated from Ulster in large numbers to escape religious persecution and high rents. They followed the historic Great Wagon Road from Pennsylvania to North Carolina, many of them settling in Appalachia. Several of the Revolutionary heroines discussed in this book were such immigrants born on foreign shores. Some were either born in other American colonies or died in other American colonies, but because they all expressed their bravery and patriotism during their lifetime in North Carolina, they are recognized as daughters of the Old North State.

As is the case when researching historical figures, one encounters variations in the spelling of names. This is because the spelling of names was not generally standardized in America until the 1800s. Therefore, I chose to use the spellings for surnames as noted on tombstones, acknowledging that it sometimes differed from the spellings encountered in historic documents or secondary sources. My one exception to this rule was the puzzling case of Elizabeth Maxwell Steele whose name was spelled "Steele" in primary source documents, Daughters of the American Revolution records, and virtually every resource I encountered. Indeed, with the exception of one document, the only place it was spelled "Steel" was on her tombstone! I suppose that is the exception that proves the rule. In cases where research revealed discrepancies about dates of birth and death, I once again chose to use the dates written on gravestones as my guide. This choice was made solely because it provided a way for me to ground my research in a common format.

The Role of Women in Colonial North Carolina

The lives of women in eighteenth-century North Carolina centered around fulfilling the duties of hearth and home. Young girls were trained to this end by an education focused on the domestic arts which included sewing, cooking, overseeing the household, and caring for children. Once married, women became subject to their husbands financially and legally.

Upon marriage, a woman's property and personal possessions became part of her husband's estate, and there were no laws that guaranteed she would ever recover these even after her husband's death. Women were awarded one-third of their husband's real estate after his death, but all other property could be awarded to their children. Marriage placed women in the seventeenth century at a distinct legal disadvantage.

It is not surprising that women in colonial North Carolina sometimes sought to exact marriage contracts that would figure to their advantage economically. Marriage contracts could be widely divergent in their content, and while it was possible to fashion these contracts to a certain advantage prior to marriage, women had no recourse to altering them once the marriage was accomplished. Interestingly, the great majority of these contracts were entered into by widows, suggesting that these women were already property owners seeking to protect their assets.

Marriage contracts in North Carolina during the colonial era represented a departure in legal tone from others in the southern colonies which sought to maintain property within the family from which it originated. In North Carolina, most marriage contracts granted only limited powers to the prospective wife concerning the property she possessed at the time the marriage was contracted or concerning that which she would receive after the marriage. Therefore, it was in a woman's best interests to protect her current property as well as her future economic stability.

According to the North Carolina Higher-Court Records of 1702-1708, a widow by the name of Anne Walker, upon learning that her prospective husband owned no real estate, obliged him to will to her the sum of £500 as a hedge against a destitute widowhood. In Northampton County, one John Dawson willed that his assets be used to fulfill the terms of his prenuptial agreement including his cattle, gold, silver, and debts owed to him. Peter Avent, also of Northampton County, willed to his wife £300 to fulfill the terms of the contract made at his marriage.

Other North Carolina marriage contracts of the time focused upon the assurance that, upon widowhood, wives would be able to provide for their children from former or future marriages. New Hanover County deeds books of that time relate that one Sarah Watson asked that her future husband apply one half of her late husband's estate to support a child by a former marriage. Another woman by the name of Elizabeth Rowan requested that the slaves and silver from her husband's will be divided among the children of her previous marriage.

Upon widowhood, women were often forced to find employment. Out of necessity, they depended upon those domestic talents they had exercised throughout their lives. These might include sewing, washing, cooking or teaching. Those whose husbands had been merchants or plantation owners sought to continue their husband's businesses in order to survive financially. This was not an easy proposition since it involved the management of employees or slaves, the planting and harvesting of crops, managing a payroll and various other business operations.

One profitable enterprise for widows was tavern keeping, though it was a potentially dangerous occupation for a woman and fraught with legal difficulties. The court minutes of New Hanover County found Lettice Blackmore and Elizabeth Sanders guilty of "keeping disorderly houses, & harbouring & detaining Common Sailors," a fact which proved to be problematic to merchants and sea captains trading on the Cape Fear River. Their tavern licenses were revoked and they were warned against the future serving of liquor to sailors or other rambunctious customers.

Another profitable enterprise for widows in North Carolina was ferry keeping. Ferries were maintained by women in Cumberland, Tyrell, New Hanover, Bertie, and Beaufort counties.

Unlike married women, single women, widows, and spinsters enjoyed numerous freedoms under the law and were recognized as individuals for the purpose of executing contracts and deeds, making wills, bringing lawsuits, administering estates and acting as guardians. An unattached woman who conducted her financial business wisely was often in a position preferable to that of a married woman who was subject to her husband financially, socially and legally. Not surprisingly, some women chose to remain single and thereby maintain the control of their property and personal liberty.

Another topic entirely was the role and treatment of female indentured servants, apprentices and orphans during the colonial period. Though married women of the time in North Carolina were subject to their husbands both socially and legally, they fared better than indentured servants, apprentices or orphans. Women who lived as indentured servants were often newcomers to the Carolina colony and rarely had family connections to protect them in their role as servants. Furthermore, they were subject to a contract which guided the term of their indenture and which could be harsh in its terms. Depending upon the wording of their contract these women could be bought, sold, or bequeathed as property until the term of their indenture was fulfilled. They were sometimes subject to severe punishment and received little notice in the legal system although the courts could demand the sale of an indentured servant deemed to be excessively mistreated. In such instances, a servant could be sold to the highest bidder with the proceeds being used to pay court costs. The remainder of the servant's indenture would be expected to be fulfilled.

Seeking freedom from their restricted lives, servants were frequently reported as runaways and were subject to capture and return to their masters. Indentured servants could not marry without the permission of their master, and the penalty for bearing an illegitimate child while indentured was to add one or two years to the term of indenture, presumably in reparation for the service time lost in caring for a child. Women who had two or three illegitimate children during the term of their indenture might find their time of servitude nearly doubled.

Upon the completion of their period of servitude, "freedom dues" were bestowed upon former servants which reflected the basic necessities of life during the colonial period. In 1715, freedom dues included three barrels of Indian corn and two suits of clothes, according to North Carolina State Records. By 1741, the allotment had been reduced to £3 and one suit of clothing. On occasion, county courts were more generous and required masters to provide more substantial awards for servants who had fulfilled their contractual obligations. According to the Rowan County Court Minutes of 1772 and 1774, Nansey Queen was required to be supplied with a cow and calf, a mare, a spinning wheel with a pair of cards, and a set of knitting needles. Another indentured servant named Agnes Williams, upon separation from her master, received a cow and calf, a Bible and a spinning wheel. In the Tryon County Court Minutes of 1774, two female indentured servants were awarded £3, a bed, a cow and calf, a ewe and lamb, and a spinning wheel as freedom dues. Both liberated servants and apprentices were subject to such freedom dues.

Apprentices were orphans without sufficient financial resources to ensure guardianship. They were attached by order of the county courts to masters who agreed to support and train them until they reached the age of majority. Apprentices could be discharged from the guardianship of their masters and mistresses by the court in cases where it was determined that their circumstances were inadequate or even dangerous. Female orphans and apprentices of the time were expected to be schooled in reading, particularly in reading the Bible and classics, and various female accomplishments such as sewing, cooking, and other domestic duties.

In colonial times, the wealthy were more likely to learn to write as well as read, though the only systematic education for women to be found in colonial North Carolina resided in the Moravian settlements at Bethabara and Friedberg. These schools originated shortly before the Revolution and focused on teaching boys and girls Bible stories, religious catechism, reading, writing and arithmetic. In 1802, the Moravians would institute Salem College for the education of women.

Women in skilled trades could be found in the North Carolina colony prior to the Revolution. The most common of these trades was spinning and it was to be found particularly in the backcountry which could be defined as that region of North Carolina which included both the mountain region and the piedmont. Women could even be said to have held the sole production rights to spinning since it was considered the work of a woman and not likely to be undertaken by any male.

Weaving was the most widely practiced trade in the colony of North Carolina, and the spinning of women was necessary to provide fibers for this trade to local weavers. Women apprentices often received spinning wheels upon the completion of their indenture. In the case of married women, their husbands owned the spinning wheels and any related equipment. Upon their death, men usually willed the spinning wheels operated throughout a lifetime by women to their wife or daughter.

It is astounding to realize that the Revolutionary heroines of North Carolina achieved their courageous stature within the confines of a society which placed rigid restrictions upon their behavior. These women brought the training of a lifetime in caring for others to the patriotic deeds which they performed in the cause of American independence. It is not because of their conformity to the societal strictures of their day, but in spite of it, that they prevailed heroically in their defense of hearth and home.

Penelope Padgett Barker

Penelope Padgett (1728-1796) was born in Edenton, North Carolina, the daughter of Samuel and Elizabeth Blount Padgett. Her father was a physician and planter, and her mother was the daughter of eminent politician and planter James Blount. Penelope had two sisters, Elizabeth and Sarah. During her teenage years, Penelope lost both her father and her sister Elizabeth. It became Penelope's responsibility to care for the three children of her deceased sister and she married their father, attorney John Hodgson, in 1745. Hodgson had been made legatee of her father's estate. Two sons were born to John and Penelope, Samuel and Thomas, before their father died in 1747.

At the age of nineteen, Penelope Padgett Hodgson was caregiver to five children and manager of the Hodgson plantations in eastern North Carolina. As a young, wealthy widow and a member of society, it was not surprising that Penelope would marry again in 1751 a prominent politician and landowner named James Craven. No children were born of their brief union, and Craven died four years later in 1755 leaving his entire estate to Penelope. At the age of twenty-seven, Penelope was left to manage large holdings of property and to care for her children and the children of her sister.

Thomas Barker, an attorney originally from Massachusetts, had moved to Bertie County, North Carolina in 1735. Thomas and Penelope were married in 1757. By 1774, Barker had become a prominent member of eastern North Carolina society and served as the Treasurer of the Province of North Carolina and Clerk of the Assembly. Three children were born to Thomas and Penelope Padgett Barker, none of whom survived the first year of life. In 1761, Penelope was once again forced to care for family members and property when her husband's political career required that he move to London to serve as agent for the North Carolina colony. With the outbreak of the American Revolution, and the blockading of American ports, Thomas Barker would not return to Penelope and the colonies until September 1778. During his absence, Penelope continued in her role as a prominent matron in Edenton society, taking part in the social functions acceptable to a woman of her class and time.

The tea party, in colonial America, reflected the social dominance of Great Britain over the colonies and was the most acceptable form of social gathering of the time. The drinking of tea was a genteel pastime, providing guests an opportunity to exchange social pleasantries and to promote continued financial support for Britain by consuming tremendous amounts of tea imported from India. When Parliament passed the Tea Act of 1773, the British East India Tea Company was given sole rights to sell tea to the American colonies. The British East India Tea Company suffered from crushing debt and owed the Crown in excess of £400,000 incurred yearly from contractual payments. Additionally, the social and political climate in India was creating economic instability for the company, and further financial losses had resulted from the French and Indian War. By enacting legislation which guaranteed a monopoly on the sale of tea to the colonies, the Crown was assured of collecting its yearly revenue. Though the Tea Act was not designed to antagonize the colonists, it was the final piece of legislation in a long line of political acts which infuriated colonists who resisted the imposition of a monopoly designed to fund the Crown at their expense. This piece of legislation inspired the Boston Tea Party in which members of the outlawed Sons of Liberty dressed as Mohawk Indians and boarded three British ships anchored in Boston harbor in December 1773, dumping 92,000 pounds of tea overboard.

Ten months after the infamous Boston Tea Party, on October 25, 1774, Penelope Padgett Barker, together with fifty other ladies of like mind, met at the house of Elizabeth King, the wife of an Edenton merchant, and vowed to uphold their loyalty to their husbands, brothers, and the American colonies by refusing to continue serving tea or to wear clothing produced from British cloth. As proof of their dedication to the cause, they drew up a list of resolves:

"We, the ladyes of Edenton, do hereby solemnly engage not to conform to ye pernicious Custom of Drinking Tea, or that we, the aforesaid Ladyes, will not promote ye wear of any manufacture from England, until such time that all Acts which tend to enslave this our Native Country shall be repealed." The ladies further declared they were "determined to give memorable proof of their patriotism" and refused to be "indifferent on any occasion that appears nearly to affect the peace and happiness of our country." They stated it "was a duty that we owe, not only to our near and dear connections…but to ourselves." The Edenton Resolves was sent to a newspaper in London.

Political resistance, especially in the climate leading up to the American Revolution, was not uncommon. But political resistance by women was unprecedented in the western world, and Europe was stunned by news of the Edenton Tea Party. A political cartoon of the Edenton Tea Party was published in the *Morning Chronicle and London Advertiser* in March 1775. Ridiculed by the British because it was a political statement made by women, the Edenton Tea Party, at least among the British, did not match the uproar caused by the Boston Tea Party though the political message was identical. In the colonies, however, Penelope Padgett Barker was praised for her resistance to the Crown, and colonial women began to boycott British goods as a result of her daring initiative.

Penelope Padgett Barker led a quieter life in Edenton after the Revolution was over. Thomas Barker died in 1789, and Penelope died in 1796. Both are buried in the Johnson Family Cemetery at Hayes Plantation near Edenton.

Martha McFarlane Bell

Martha "Mattie" McFarlane (1735-1820) was born in what is present-day Orange County, North Carolina. There is little information about her parents, but her surname indicates that she was of Scots-Irish origin. She was a devout Presbyterian and a woman of strong mind and determination. At all hours of the day and night she served as a nurse and midwife to families throughout the county.

Martha McFarlane married Colonel John McGee, a successful landowner, merchant and widower around 1759. Colonel McGee had been granted a large tract of land in Orange County in 1753. He built a gristmill there at the headwaters of Sandy Creek and operated an ordinary. In colonial days, an "ordinary" would be defined as any tavern or inn that provided a meal at a fixed price. The location of his ordinary took advantage of trading routes which ran between frontier settlements farther west and established Virginia townships.

Children born to John McGee and Martha McFarlane McGee included Jane McGee Welborn; Susannah McGee Mendenhall; the Reverend John McGee, a Methodist minister; the Reverend William McGee, a Presbyterian minister; and Andrew McGee.

After McGee's death, Martha married William Bell, who became the first sheriff of Randolph County in 1779, clerk of court, and later a member of the North Carolina General Assembly. William Bell operated a gristmill in the Deep River Community which became a popular gathering place for Whigs to discuss the politics of the day.

Martha McFarlane Bell is remembered for an incident which took place after the Battle of Guilford Courthouse in March 1781. Lord Cornwallis paid a visit to Bell's Mill with his troops in order to rest and reorganize his men between engagements. He decided that the mill would be a safe and useful place to obtain provisions and ground corn meal to feed his troops. Mrs. Bell managed to wrest a promise from Lord Cornwallis that he would ensure the safety of her home and mill during his stay of two or three days. During this time, Martha McFarlane Bell kept a diary. Cornwallis' visit was the perfect opportunity for her to be the eyes and ears of the patriots, and while serving the General and his men, she listened carefully and discreetly to the information she heard.

Patriot General Harry Lee arrived with his forces after Cornwallis' departure. Mrs. Bell's information, together with her knowledge of the surrounding countryside, enabled her to provide General Lee with useful intelligence about the movements of General Cornwallis. As a result, Lee was able to stage a successful counterattack using a small band of cavalry against the greater forces of Cornwallis. As further assistance, Mrs. Bell's itinerant nursing occupation enabled her to provide information by passing through enemy lines and reporting the movements of enemy troops.

Colonel David Fanning, a prominent Loyalist who operated in the area, was suspicious of the Bell family's Whig affiliations and activities, and launched constant and unannounced visits to the Bell home and mill in hopes of catching William Bell in the act of treason. These visits became so frequent William Bell elected to spend months at a time away from home, either in hiding or out riding with patriot troops. Martha Bell took care of the farm, home, mill and the children during these periods. On one visit in 1781, Colonel Fanning threatened to kill the Bell family and burn the house, but the family made such a show of strength that Fanning reneged and permitted the Bell family and property to remain unharmed.

Martha's son John attended Dr. David Caldwell's Academy, a prominent school in Guilford County which trained future Presbyterian ministers and prominent politicians of the day. At some point along the way, John was converted to the Methodist faith. As a staunch Presbyterian, Martha Bell was opposed to her son John's conversion to Methodism but relented when John's brother William, who became a Presbyterian minister, convinced her to accept it. In fact, Martha Bell was instrumental in founding Old Union Methodist Church in Randolph County, North Carolina, the scene of some of the earliest camp meetings in the state.

Martha McFarlane Bell died in 1820, one year before her husband William. Both are buried at the Bell-Welborn Cemetery in Randolph County. She is remembered for giving aid to the patriots and providing supplies to the cause of the American Revolution. At the site of the Battle of Guilford Courthouse, a memorial dedicated to Mrs. Bell reads, "Loyal Whig, Enthusiastic Patriot, Revolutionary Heroine." She is recognized as an American patriot by both the National Society Daughters of the American Revolution and the National Society Sons of the American Revolution.

"Martha Bell
Consort of Wm. Bell
Departed This Life
Sept. 9, 1820
Aged 85 Years"

Above: "Mrs. Martha McFarlane McGee-Bell
1735-1820
Loyal Whig – Enthusiastic Patriot
Revolutionary Heroine.
We are dedicated to E.W. Caruthers For the Eventful Story of Her Life
Erected by
Alexander Martin Chapter D.A.R.
High Point, N.C.
1928"

Below: "Revolutionary War Patriot
Martha McFarlane McGee Bell
Born 1735
Died September 9, 1820 in N.C.
Marker Placed by Guilford Battle Chapter NSDAR
September 14, 1997"

Hannah Millikan Blair

Hannah Millikan Blair's religious affiliation is central to the story of her contributions as a patriot during the American Revolution. As a Quaker, Hannah demonstrated an abiding sense of fairness, introspection, and social discernment which typified the American Quaker movement during the eighteenth century. Her bravery, though steadfast and real, was not born of defiance but, rather, out of a sense of service and faith.

Quakers, or the Society of Friends, in 18th century America adhered to a doctrine of peace which prohibited them from participating in war or violence, either by serving as a soldier or donating money to the cause of war. They were particularly persecuted for this refusal to participate in the American Revolution, often being identified with Tories as the enemy. Prior to the outbreak of the Revolution, Quakers were secure in decrying the unjustness of excessive taxation or debating the of issue of slavery. In fact, many Quakers in good standing had freed their slaves and demanded the fair treatment of Native Americans by the time of the American Revolution. But as war with Great Britain approached, Quakers faced the dilemma of choosing between their desire to protect their colonies and their belief that participation in war could not be justified. When the inevitability of war became certain, Quakers withdrew from public office and ceased their rhetoric about contentious political subjects which they believed to be inflammatory. Those of their members who joined the armed forces were often disowned by the Society.

Hannah Millikan (1756-1852) was the youngest child of William Millikan, the first Register of Deeds of Randolph County, North Carolina, and Jane White Blair, who were married in Chester County, Pennsylvania. As a young child, Hannah's family moved from Pennsylvania to Deep River, North Carolina, in Randolph County. Hannah married Enos Blair and they had thirteen children, twelve of whom survived to adulthood. Hannah's patriotic contributions during the Revolution persisted even as she gave birth to one child per year during the American Revolution.

Hannah Millikan Blair was known for providing food, supplies and medicine to patriot soldiers who were in hiding from Tories. She carried messages back and forth for patriots, mended their clothes, and hid them in her home from the enemy.

During the Revolution, Tories searching for two patriots were outwitted by Hannah who hid the men in a corn crib, heaped corn on top of them, and stood nearby industriously shucking corn as the soldiers searched. On another occasion, she tore open the corner of a featherbed tick and shoved a visiting patriot inside among the feathers, quickly gesturing for Colonel David Fanning and his Loyalist soldiers to look under the bed to prove that no one was hiding there. Hannah then sat down calmly to mend the feather tick, declaring, "Thee may search as thee pleases."

Simon Dixon, a Quaker miller from Pennsylvania, found his way to North Carolina during the Quaker migration of the mid-1700s. In 1753, he constructed a rock dam on Cane Creek after which he built a grist mill in what is now the Snow Camp and Cane Creek area. The mill operated using millstones Dixon brought with him from Pennsylvania. As immigrants trickled in from Pennsylvania, Dixon built a general store nearby to supply their needs. A skirmish between patriots and Tories took place at Dixon's Mill in 1779. Hannah sought out the patriot soldiers who were hiding in the area and took food to them. When confronted by the Tories who demanded to know where the patriots were hiding, Hannah explained that she had taken food to a sick neighbor several miles away and did not know the whereabouts of the patriots. The Tories, unable to confirm their suspicions, released Hannah. The Dixon home was taken over by General Cornwallis in 1781, one week after the Battle of Guilford Courthouse. It became a British headquarters while Dixon and his family were forced to find shelter elsewhere.

After the Revolution, Hannah was formally thanked by the new government and awarded a pension in recognition of the patriotic services she rendered during the conflict.

Hannah Millikan Blair was buried in the cemetery at Springfield Friends Meeting House in High Point. Legend says the name of "Springfield" derived from seven springs which were located in the field beyond the hilltop where the meeting house now stands. The first worship service at Springfield took place in 1773, and the property where the current meeting house stands was purchased in 1786. A single gravestone marks the grave of Hannah Millikan Blair's husband, Enos, and herself. The first names of their twelve children are listed below her name.

Gravesite of Hannah Blair and her husband, Enos Blair,
Springfield Friends Meeting House Cemetery, Guilford County.

Rachel Craighead Caldwell

Rachel Brown Craighead Caldwell (1739-1835) was the daughter of a prominent Presbyterian minister, Alexander Craighead, and his wife Jane Agnes Brown. Her husband, David Caldwell, was also a prominent Presbyterian minister. If the women of the American Revolution were defined in large measure by the men in their lives, it may be said that Rachel Caldwell was doubly so.

The Reverend Alexander Craighead was born in County Donegal, Ulster. At the age of seven, his parents, Thomas (Sr.), also a Presbyterian minister, his wife Margaret Craighead, and his older brother, Thomas, emigrated to America. Alexander Craighead was the pastor of the Sugar Creek Congregation and a central figure in the schism that occurred within the Presbyterian Church in colonial America. Craighead was a New Side Revivalist Presbyterian whose fiery sermons were heard in many of the original thirteen colonies and whose religious pamphlets were published by Benjamin Franklin. He is remembered for violating the Itinerant Minister Act of 1737 which forbade itinerant preaching by ministers who had not earned a college degree or who had failed to be credentialed to preach the faith. The issue was largely one of methodology. Craighead is also regarded as the spiritual father of the Mecklenburg Declaration of Independence, a document arising from the politics of Mecklenburg County, North Carolina, and reputed to be the first declaration of independence of the American colonies from British rule, preceding Thomas Jefferson's Declaration of Independence.

Born in Lancaster County, Pennsylvania, Rachel's family emigrated south when the violence of the French and Indian War (1754-1763) brought upheaval to their doorstep. Living in an isolated area and subject to frequent attacks by Indians, Rachel once declared that as soon as the family fled from one door of the house, the Indians would burst in through the other door. The family took the Great Wagon Road south from Pennsylvania into the Carolinas, the same trail that so many other Scots-Irish had followed in the settling of what came to be known as the backcountry of North Carolina.

Rachel married Dr. David Stewart Caldwell in 1766. Caldwell was a graduate of Princeton and the founder of Buffalo Presbyterian Church and Alamance Presbyterian Church, both in Guilford County. He was a minister, educator, farmer, physician and statesman. Caldwell established Dr. David Caldwell's Log College in 1767 which educated young men in theology and the classics. It came to be one of the most respected schools in the South as evidenced by the number of its graduates who became governors, congressmen, lawyers, judges, physicians and ministers. Already an educated minister, the Reverend Caldwell became a self-taught and practicing physician by studying medical textbooks brought from Philadelphia. His medical practice served his flock who had no other source of medical assistance. In addition, Caldwell turned to farming to supplement his meager minister's salary and was eventually able to successfully operate a plantation on 550 acres of land which he cultivated.

Dr. Caldwell was an active statesman who was an outspoken proponent of American independence. He represented Guilford County at the Halifax Provincial Congress, one of a series of five congresses which provided a revolutionary governmental structure in North Carolina. These congresses served the colony by providing for the organization of an army, by financing the war, and by writing the constitution and bill of rights which would help to establish the state. Caldwell was also a representative at the Hillsborough Constitutional Convention of 1788 which insisted that the United States government have a formal Bill of Rights attached to its Constitution.

Dr. Caldwell was relentlessly hunted by the British as a felon for his role in American independence, often escaping by seemingly miraculous means. On one occasion, he was captured while visiting his home and British soldiers surrounded him. As soldiers ransacked the house, and two guards were left to stand watch over Dr. Caldwell, Rachel leaned forward quietly and asked her husband, "Isn't it time for Gillespie and his men to arrive?" Overheard by one of the soldiers, she was frantically questioned. Gillespie, an officer in the Guilford Militia was a name greatly feared by the Loyalists in the county. The enemy departed hastily, leaving Dr. Caldwell, his family and his house unscathed.

In the fall of 1780, a stranger appeared one night at the door of Rachel Caldwell's home. Weary and hungry, the stranger asked for food and lodging saying he had official papers for General Nathaniel Greene and he believed he would be safe at the home of a minister. Mrs. Caldwell warned him that their home was not a safe harbor because it was constantly surveilled by Loyalists who were suspicious of her husband's political views. She advised the stranger that she would feed him, but that he must eat and depart quickly for his own safety. At that moment, Mrs. Caldwell heard shouts demanding that the house be surrounded. She quickly led the stranger out through the other side of the house and pointed to a leafy locust tree which she told him to climb up into and hide. While Tories plundered the house, the patriot crouched in the foliage of the locust tree, shielded by the dark night. After their departure, he climbed down and passed on through the night to deliver his important papers to General Greene.

Lord Cornwallis invaded Guilford County in 1781, learning soon afterward about the activities of Dr. David Caldwell, an ardent patriot. Cornwallis placed a bounty of two hundred pounds on Caldwell's head, forcing him to hide out in the swamps until after the Battle of Guilford Courthouse. Cornwallis' soldiers paid a visit to the Caldwell home, pretending to be patriots though a servant had spotted them from afar in their red uniforms and warned Rachel of their approach. Mrs. Caldwell, on the pretext of leaving to attend to her children, went to warn two neighbors in hiding that the troops of Cornwallis were present, permitting the neighbors to escape. When Mrs. Caldwell returned to accuse the soldiers of being redcoats rather than patriots, they told her they were taking her house over as a headquarters and demanded that she and her family depart. She took her children to the smokehouse to live for several days where they ate dried fruit which she had managed to confiscate on her way out. She and her children were frequently insulted, taunted and threatened by British soldiers during their stay in the smokehouse. When Mrs. Caldwell asked for protection for herself and her children, she was told that women were regarded as rebels just as their men were. Before leaving, the commanding officer ordered that Dr. Caldwell's private papers, sermons, the family Bible, valuable manuscripts and the contents of his library be burned outdoors while his wife and children looked on. When the troops departed, it was discovered that the family's food stores had been depleted, and even the fenceposts on the property had been either burned or confiscated. According to legend, the only creature left alive on the property was an old goose.

The Caldwell house remained under suspicion and was subjected to frequent searches by the British. On one such occasion, a soldier grabbed an elegant tablecloth, given to Mrs. Caldwell by her mother, from a chest of drawers. She immediately let out a cry and began a tug of war with him over the tablecloth. Seeing that a battle of strength was not in her favor, she cried out to the other soldiers and asked if none of them had wives or daughters for the sake of whom they would intervene. One man stepped up and demanded that the soldier relinquish the tablecloth into the hands of Mrs. Caldwell. When the man grudgingly did so, the British cheered for the courage of Rachel Caldwell.

Rachel Craighead Caldwell is remembered as an American patriot by both the National Society Daughters of the American Revolution and the National Society Sons of the American Revolution. She rests in the cemetery of the Buffalo Presbyterian Church which her husband founded in Guilford County, North Carolina. Under her headstone are also buried the remains of Mary Jane Caldwell who died in 1852. Dr. David Caldwell is also buried in Buffalo Presbyterian Church Cemetery.

Buffalo Presbyterian Church in Guilford County, founded by Reverend David Caldwell., husband of Rachel Caldwell.

"Sacred to the memory of
Rachel Caldwell
born in Lancaster Co Pa
daughter of Alexander Craighead
Consort of the Rev David Caldwell DD
who departed this life June 12 1835

ALSO
under this stone the remains of
Mary Jane Caldwell
daughter of J & M Caldwell
who departed this life July 6 1832
aged 4 years & 6 months"

Sarah Robinson Erwin

Sarah Anne Robinson (1750-1782) was born in Catawba County, North Carolina, to James and Catherine Sherrill Robinson who were originally from South Carolina. In 1770, Sarah Robinson married Alexander Erwin, a notable patriot from Morganton, Burke County. Their children were Catherine Erwin who married an Erwin first cousin; Mary "Polly" Erwin who married Presbyterian minister John McKamie Wilson; James Erwin who married Margaret Phifer; Margaret "Peggy" Erwin who married Hugh Tate; Hannah Erwin and Joseph Erwin. Hannah Erwin married Major Zebulon Baird and their grandsons were Zebulon Baird Vance, North Carolina Governor (1862-1865), and Robert Brank Vance, a Confederate general and United States Congressman.

Colonel Alexander Erwin (1750-1829, the Scots-Irish son of a Presbyterian minister, was born in Bucks County, Pennsylvania, and moved to Rowan County (present-day Burke County) shortly before the American Revolution. He resided at Cherry Fields, the home of his parents located east of Upper Creek. Alexander Erwin was a planter, a politician, and a soldier. He was among the patriots who fought and defeated Major Patrick Ferguson at the Battle of Kings Mountain in 1780. He subsequently fought at the Battle of Cowpens in January 1781 and at the Battles of Cowan's Ford and Tarrant's Tavern, both in February 1781. Erwin would earn the rank of colonel in the Burke County Militia.

Alexander Erwin served as the first clerk of the Court of Pleas and Quarter Sessions, was appointed an auditor for claims made against the state arising from militia pay, was appointed one of the original trustees of the Morgan Academy which served as the first institution of learning in Burke County, and was a member of the North Carolina House of Commons from 1793-1797 and in 1804.

Colonel Erwin was known for his abiding hatred of Tories. Even after the end of the American Revolution, Tories were permitted in Morganton only during the times when court was in session in Burke County. Colonel Erwin stood on the steps every morning that court was in session and declared that all Tories must depart Morganton by sundown or be forcibly removed. As the story goes, Erwin was never disobeyed in this declaration.

Alexander Erwin had good reason to despise the Tories. While he was away fighting the British, the war came to Alexander Erwin's own doorstep. Erwin's wife Sarah Robinson Erwin came to the aid of a wounded friend and neighbor by the name of Samuel Alexander who had been severely wounded by the enemy in the cause of American independence. Mrs. Erwin sheltered him in an outbuilding, hoping to hide him from marauding Tory forces until he could heal. A band of Tories searching for Whigs at the Erwin home disregarded the protests of Sarah Erwin and plundered the Erwin home. When they proceeded to the outbuilding where Samuel Alexander lay, Sarah Erwin blocked the door. They shoved her aside and flung open the door to discover the helpless Alexander. As a sword was raised to strike him down, Sarah Erwin threw herself over the wounded man's body to protect him and received the full blow of the sword on her right arm. It is not clear if Sarah Erwin's arm was terribly mangled or actually cut off, but she never recovered from the effects of the attack. She died in 1785 at the age of thirty-four.

Brave Sarah Robinson Erwin is remembered for her heroic patriotism by both the National Society Daughters of the American Revolution and the National Society Sons of the American Revolution. She and her husband are buried beside of one another at Quaker Meadows Cemetery in Morganton, Burke County, an historic cemetery which holds the remains of nine Revolutionary War patriots.

The grave of Sarah Robinson Erwin at Quaker Meadows Cemetery in Burke County.

Elizabeth Hutchinson Jackson

Elizabeth Hutchinson Jackson (1737-1781) was born in Larne, County Antrim, Ulster, in present-day Northern Ireland. She married Andrew Jackson (Sr.) in 1761, who was born in Carrickfergus, County Antrim. They emigrated to America in 1765 with their two oldest sons, Hugh and Robert, to escape religious persecution and the exorbitant tariffs of the English imposed upon the North Irish.

They traveled down the Great Wagon Road from Pennsylvania to the Waxhaw Settlement which was located between the borderlands of North and South Carolina. There they acquired two hundred acres of inferior farmland along Twelve Mile Creek, near the Catawba River.

Elizabeth Jackson was the mother of three sons: Hugh Jackson (1763-1779) who died at the Battle of Stono Ferry in South Carolina during the Revolution; Robert Jackson (1764-1781) who was held as a prison of war by the British and died of smallpox at the age of seventeen; and Andrew Jackson (Jr.) (1767-1845) who was the 7th President of the United States and who fought at the Battle of Hanging Rock during the American Revolution, the Battles of Talladega and Horseshoe Bend in the Creek Wars, and in the Battles of Pensacola and New Orleans during the War of 1812. Andrew Jackson (Jr.) was born shortly after the Jackson family arrived in the Waxhaws, only three weeks after the untimely death of his father at the age of twenty-nine.

Elizabeth Hutchinson Jackson was left a widow with three young children and no means of support. She moved into the home of her invalid sister Jane and brother-in-law, James Crawford, in order to nurse her sister and to ensure support for herself and her children.

Elizabeth's sons were eager to fight in the Revolution when it broke out, having been entertained throughout their childhood with tales of their family's battles with the British in the siege of Carrickfergus. Though the Revolutionary War took several years to move into the southern colonies, the brothers would have the opportunity to experience firsthand the horrors of the infamous Waxhaw Massacre.

In 1780, the British launched an attack upon South Carolina, capturing the port city of Charleston, and stirring up dissent between Patriots and Loyalists. The countryside underwent widespread looting and murder. Over one hundred patriots were slaughtered, with many bodies found mutilated. Approximately one hundred and fifty wounded patriots were brought to the church at Waxhaw where local settlers tended to them including the family of Elizabeth Jackson. Not long afterward, young Andrew Jackson and his brothers would join a patriot regiment, and Hugh Jackson would die at the Battle of Stono Ferry from heat exhaustion.

Andrew and Robert would serve under Colonel William Davie at the Battle of Hanging Rock and would eventually be captured by the British at the home of a relative, Thomas Crawford, in 1781. When a British officer commanded Andrew to clean his boots, the youth refused and the officer struck him with his sword. In attempting to fend off the blow, Andrew Jackson's hand and face were slashed and he bore the scars for the remainder of his life. His brother, Robert, was also struck with a sword when he, too, refused to clean the boots of the officer. Both were imprisoned and held at Camden, contracted smallpox, and subsisted on the scanty provisions that were given them by the British. Elizabeth Jackson managed to secure their release through an exchange of prisoners, and the dying Robert rode with his mother while Andrew walked alongside them for forty miles to Waxhaw. Robert died within a few days of returning home, and Andrew was unable to leave his own sickbed for weeks.

When her only son Andrew recovered, Elizabeth Jackson volunteered to nurse sick prisoners of war who were held aboard two ships in Charleston harbor after an outbreak of cholera. She contracted the disease herself and died a few months later. Left an orphan at the age of fourteen, a bitter Andrew Jackson would forever after blame the British for the death of his mother and brothers.

Elizabeth Hutchinson Jackson was buried in a simple unmarked grave on a hillside near Charleston. A friend, Agnes Barton, dressed her in her best dress and Mr. Barton made the casket where they placed her body for burial. Though Andrew Jackson insisted that he would someday find his mother's remains and bury her near her family, he was never able to do so. Not until 1949 was a marker placed to commemorate Elizabeth Hutchinson Jackson at the Old Waxhaw Presbyterian Cemetery in Lancaster County, South Carolina. A memorial to Elizabeth Hutchinson Jackson, erected by the Catawba Chapter Daughters of the American Revolution also stands in the cemetery. These are the words that commemorate her patriotism:

"Erected to the memory of Elizabeth Hutchinson Jackson,
mother of Andrew Jackson Seventh President of the United States."

"It was her zeal for accomplishment that made handicaps seem to resolve themselves in her favor which enabled them to endure the hardships of the Great Wagon Road to the garden of the Waxhaws."

"Elizabeth Hutchinson, wife of Andrew Jackson, Sr., of Larne, County Antrim, Ireland. Settled in Waxhaws, 1765. While nursing Waxhaw patriots on a British prison ship in Charleston, S.C., Elizabeth was stricken with small-pox. Died November 1781.
Buried Near Charleston, S.C."

"Last words to her son: 'Make friends by being honest, keep them by being steadfast.
Never tell a lie--nor take what is not your own--nor sue for slander.'"

Erected by Catawba Chapter D.A.R. 1949

Memorial to Elizabeth Hutchinson Jackson
Old Waxhaw Presbyterian Cemetery
Lancaster County, South Carolina

Old Waxhaw Presbyterian Church, 1896

Grace Greenlee McDowell

Grace Grizzell Greenlee was the daughter of two prominent pioneer families, the Greenlees and the McDowells. Her father, James Greenlee (1707-1757), was born in Ulster (present-day Northern Ireland) and settled in Pennsylvania.

In 1735, a land promoter by the name of Benjamin Borden received 100,000 acres along the James River in the upper Shenandoah Valley. The land was received by grant through the governor's Council under Lieutenant Governor William Gooch (Sir William Gooch) of Virginia. Legend says that this generous grant was obtained by gifting Lieutenant Governor Gooch with a buffalo calf. The grant stipulated that one family must be settled for every 1,000 acres given, requiring Borden to draw 100 families to the Shenandoah Valley in order to take possession of the land. By 1739, Borden had laid right to his claim by receiving a patent for 92,100 acres which had come to be called the Borden Tract.

James Greenlee became a beneficiary of the Borden grant which covered much of Augusta and Rockbridge Counties when he volunteered to settle in the Shenandoah Valley from his Pennsylvania home and to bring other families of Scots and Scots-Irish heritage to settle in the area. James Greenlee settled in Rockbridge County with his wife Mary Elizabeth McDowell. Their cabin was located by a spring near present day Fairfield. They sold the property, purchased another plot of land from Mary's brother James McDowell, and operated a tavern near Timber Ridge until James Greenlee's death in 1757. Mary continued to operate the tavern for another seventeen years before moving in with her son and assisting him in running a ferry across the James River. He is buried in the McDowell-McElrath Presbyterian Church Cemetery, located one mile north of Morganton, North Carolina.

Grace McDowell's mother, Mary Elizabeth McDowell (1707-1809), wife of James Greenlee, was a colorful and eccentric character. Like her husband, Mary was born in Northern Ireland, emigrated to America with her family, and married her husband around 1736 in Cumberland County, Pennsylvania. They moved from Pennsylvania to the Shenandoah Valley and she became the first white woman to settle in Rockbridge County, Virginia, as stated on her tombstone located on the farm of her son, David Greenlee. Believed by many to be a witch, she was regarded warily by both white settlers and the Indians who believed she was crazy. As a consequence, she was allowed to roam freely in and out of Indian camps for fear that denying her might incur reprisals. There is no evidence that Mary McDowell Greenlee was ever tried as a witch, though tales abound of her suspicious activities. As proof of the fear and respect she generated, she was allowed to rescue with impunity a young white child named Alice Lewis, a relative, kidnapped by the Indians and residing in their camp. Disputes among court officers in Rockbridge County were settled by Mary

McDowell Greenlee at the age of 99 out of respect for her memory and her person regarding ownership of land tracts dating back to the 1730s and 1740s. Her memory of county history assisted in preserving the record of the earliest white settlers to Rockbridge County.

Grace Grizell Greenlee McDowell (1750-1823), exemplified the feisty spirit and courage of her forebears. Born in Rockbridge County, Virginia, she married Captain John Bowman of Frederick County, Virginia, in 1778. Bowman was killed at the Battle of Ramsour's Mill, Lincoln County, NC, in 1780. Grace and John Bowman had a daughter named Mary Bowman who would marry Colonel William Allison Tate of Burke County.

Grace's second marriage was to General Charles McDowell (1743-1815) in 1782. McDowell was a Whig officer in the Revolutionary War who, with his brother Joseph, served under General Griffith Rutherford in the campaign against the Cherokee. In 1776 the Cherokee demanded the withdrawal of settlers from Indian lands in North Carolina, and when their demands were not met they attacked and killed settlers along the frontier. In reprisal, General Rutherford set out with 2,500 troops gathered from the western counties. They departed from Davidson's Fort, also known as Old Fort, in McDowell County, joined forces with Colonel Andrew Williamson of South Carolina, and burned thirty-six Cherokee villages.

General Charles McDowell and his brother, Major Joseph McDowell, became heroes at the Battle of Kings Mountain in 1780. British Major Patrick Ferguson issued a challenge to patriot militias in North Carolina to either lay down their arms or suffer defeat at the hands of his Loyalist troops. The Overmountain Men who were mustered in Tennessee, Virginia and North Carolina answered his call, streaming out of the mountains of Appalachia, and, uniting with militias, met up with Ferguson on Kings Mountain at the border between North and South Carolina. Charles McDowell consigned his troops to his brother Joseph before the battle, and within one hour of battle, Ferguson was killed and the Loyalist troops were resoundingly defeated.

The family of General Charles McDowell formed part of the group of pioneers who had settled in the Shenandoah Valley of Virginia under the Borden Tract. Grace Greenlee McDowell and Charles McDowell resided in Burke County on land that was known as Quaker Meadows, believed to be named after the camp of a Quaker fur trader and which bordered on frontier land populated by Indian tribes. Burke County had formerly been a part of Rowan County, a sweeping territory with an indefinite boundary. Starting in 1770, the county lines were redrawn and the westernmost section became Burke County in 1777.

Charles and Grace McDowell had four children: Captain Charles Gordon McDowell, Sarah Grace McDowell Praxton, Major General Athan McDowell, and James R. McDowell.

While General McDowell was away fighting in the Revolution, British troops assembled at the McDowell home and proceeded to round up the General's horses. As they prepared to leave, Grace Greenlee McDowell stepped up and demanded to know what they were doing. According to accounts, the soldier replied, "The King hath need of your horses," whereupon Grace McDowell drew a pistol from her skirts and shoved it in his face. The trooper immediately retracted his order, declaring, "Madam, the King hath no further need of your horses," and fled the scene leaving the horses behind.

Grace Grizell Greenlee McDowell is buried at Quaker Meadows Cemetery in

Morganton, North Carolina. She is recognized as an American patriot by the National Society Daughters of the American Revolution for manufacturing gunpowder for patriot soldiers in their fight against the British.

The gravestone of Grace Greenlee McDowell
located in Quaker Meadows Cemetery
in Burke County.

Margaret O'Neil McDowell

Margaret "Mary" O'Neil (pre-1723–post-1780) was born in Antrim, County Tyrone, Ulster (Northern Ireland). Hers was an illustrious background. Born around 1717 at Shane's Castle on Lough Neagh, she was a member of the royal house of the O'Neil clan who had built the castle in the 1300s naming it Eden-Duff-Carrick. A descendant, Shane McBrian O'Neil, renamed the castle after himself two centuries later.

The planned colonization of Northern Ireland by the British began in the 1600s in an effort to quell rebellion by the Irish against their English masters. King James I of Great Britain devised the plantation of Northern Ireland, sending colonies of Lowland Scots Presbyterians and Anglican English to settle in the six northernmost counties of Ireland. He envisioned a Protestant colony of loyal settlers who would support the Crown and help quell the unrest by their presence. But the native residents of the northern counties were rebellious and angry at their oppression by a foreign power and doubly angered by the forced presence of a new citizenry. The king's attempts to create a more civilized society did not have the desired effect.

Margaret O'Neil's proud family was Catholic, and recent settlers to the area were looked upon as the enemy. When she romantically aligned herself with Joseph McDowell (Sr.) (1715-1771), whose family were Scots Presbyterian transplants, there was intense disapproval from both families. Joseph had been trained to be a weaver in Ireland's linen industry, but rejected those prospects in favor of Margaret O'Neil. The two married in 1739 and eloped to the New World, arriving in Pennsylvania. They soon followed the Great Wagon Road of Scots-Irish immigrants flooding south, settling in the Shenandoah Valley of Virginia. There, four sons were born to Joseph and Margaret O'Neil McDowell: Hugh in 1742, Charles in 1743, John in 1751 and Joseph (Jr.) also known as "Quaker Meadows Joe" in 1756. (It should be noted that their son, General Charles McDowell, was the husband of Grace Greenlee McDowell, a Revolutionary War heroine outlined elsewhere in this book.)

Margaret's husband, Joseph McDowell (Sr.), earned the rank of Captain in the French and Indian War between 1754-1763. He and Margaret followed his relative, "Hunting John" McDowell, to North Carolina in 1761 where he received a land grant in the Quaker Meadows area of Burke County. The family settled and remained there.

No account of the American Revolution in North Carolina is complete without recounting the contributions of the McDowell's to that conflict. Joseph (Sr.) and Margaret McDowell's sons, General Charles and Major Joseph (Jr.) had served with General Griffith Rutherford in the campaign against the Cherokee in 1776, prior to fighting the British. Both were seasoned and capable warriors. Both answered the threat of British Major Patrick Ferguson who in 1780 declared that if the rebellious backcountry and mountain rebels of North Carolina did not lay down their arms and declare allegiance to the Crown, he would march across the mountains and lay waste their country with "fire and sword." Ferguson's threat was declared from Gilbert Town (now Rutherfordton), but it soon spread far and wide through the mountains of North Carolina, Tennessee and Virginia. Ferguson could scarcely have predicted his words would echo so resoundingly and, indeed, fatally, for his threat brought calamity upon his head and those of his Loyalist troops.

In response to Ferguson's words, the so-called Overmountain Men were mustered in Abingdon, Virginia, at Sycamore Shoals along the Watauga River in Tennessee, and in Elkin, North Carolina. They marched from their respective states and finally converged at Quaker Meadows at the plantation of the McDowell family. Bickering ensued over who would ultimately lead the men, and General Charles McDowell was ordered to the side of General Horatio Gates. He left his unit under the command of his brother Major Joseph McDowell (Jr.).

After several days of marching, the Overmountain Men met up with Ferguson and his Loyalists on King's Mountain near the border between North and South Carolina. They engaged Ferguson's ill-prepared forces who commanded the preeminent position at the top of the mountain. Unable to successfully aim downward at the Overmountain Men who darted behind trees and pressed forward relentlessly, the Loyalists and their leader were defeated within an hour. Ferguson was killed and 500 prisoners were taken. The victory at King's Mountain was swift and resounding. It delivered a crushing blow to the British whose luck appeared to thenceforth decline steadily up until their surrender at Yorktown. Jefferson termed the victory, "the turn of the tide of success" in the war.

Prior to the Battle of King's Mountain, Major Patrick Ferguson's soldiers had paid a visit to Quaker Meadows. They ransacked the house in the presence of Margaret O'Neil McDowell, and stole many items including the clothing of her sons Colonel Charles and Major Joseph McDowell (Jr.), knowing them to be participants in the patriot rebellion. The soldiers then taunted Mrs. McDowell, declaring they had made plans for the death of her sons. When they captured Charles, they cried, they would kill him outright. Joseph, on the other hand, they would force to his knees, make him beg for his life, and then kill him without mercy. Not easily intimidated, a woman of fearless and sharp-witted temperament, Margaret McDowell coolly replied that they had best be careful or they might be the ones doing the begging!

Scarcely a month later, the ragged, hungry and defeated rangers of the now-deceased Major Patrick Ferguson found their way back to Mrs. McDowell's home. She immediately recognized them as the threatening thieves who had plundered the McDowell's possessions and promised to murder her sons. She castigated them as "thieving, vagabond Tories." Hearing a persuasive argument of her son Major Joseph McDowell (Jr.), who had recently defeated Ferguson at the Battle of King's Mountain, she put away her anger and demonstrated her natural tendency to Christian hospitality. The enemy soldiers were given food and temporary shelter.

Margaret O'Neil McDowell is designated as an American patriot by both the National Society Daughters of the American Revolution and the National Society Sons of the American Revolution for suffering depredations by the enemy. Her grave is located in Quaker Meadows Cemetery, Burke County, along with the graves of her husband and several of her children.

Susannah Twitty Miller

Susannah "Susan" Twitty (1763-1825) was one of seven children born to Captain William John Twitty and Susannah Beller Twitty. Her father, Captain Twitty, was killed by Indians in 1775 while accompanying Daniel Boone on the Wilderness Trail to Kentucky. Their mission was to survey and cut a right-of-way from Otter Creek, Tennessee to Boonesboro, Kentucky in preparation for settlers led by Colonel Richard Henderson. The expedition was underwritten by the Transylvania Company under the leadership of Boone. Twitty was buried near the first fort built in Kentucky which was named after him, Twitty's Fort. After Twitty's death, Susannah's mother married Colonel William Graham who led troops under General Griffith Rutherford at the Battle of Moore's Creek and the Battle of Ramsour's Mill (1780).

Colonel William Graham was prominent in the cause of American independence. He was instrumental in the debates that produced the first state constitution of North Carolina, and he served as a delegate to the Fifth Provincial Congress. Known to be an ardent supporter in the cause for independence, Graham was wanted by the British. His home served as an area fort.

Eighteen forts existed in Revolutionary North Carolina. Most of them were built in the first year of the American Revolution and all but five were built in piedmont and mountain counties of North Carolina. Local residents retreated to these scattered forts along the frontier when threats of British or Indian skirmishes arose. Colonel William Graham's log house on the banks of Buffalo Creek served as one such fort and was located in Cleveland County.

By the 1780s the British were achieving little success against the colonies of the north. They decided they would turn their attention to the south in hopes of finding Loyalists to support their cause. In North Carolina, pockets of colonists still loyal to the Crown could be found in Cleveland and Rutherford Counties, and it was there that the attention of the British was drawn in their effort to put new life into the war.

In September 1780, a skirmish with Tories took place in Rutherford County. Having received prior warning that Tory raiders were in the area, local residents sought refuge at Graham's Fort. Many of them were aged or infirm, some were children, and there were others who for various reasons were unable to assist in the protection of the fort. The only men available to counter the attack were William Graham, David Dickey, and Susannah Twitty's older brother William. When the Tories demanded to be allowed admittance to the fort, William Graham refused. Approximately two dozen Tories launched an attack and demanded the surrender of the fort. Seventeen-year-old Susannah Twitty was present. When a Tory by the name of John Burke approached the fort, shoved the muzzle of his gun through a crack between the logs and fired, she pushed her brother to the floor to protect him from injury. With Susannah's encouragement, William Twitty thrust his gun through the same crack and returned fire as John Burke was reloading. Burke was struck in the head and killed. In a flash, Susannah unbolted the door and raced outside to recover Burke's gun and ammunition for the use of the patriots. The Tories retreated with their dead and wounded. Colonel Graham and the occupants of the fort departed hastily in anticipation of retaliation by the Tories. They later learned that the Tories had gathered reinforcements and returned to destroy Fort Graham.

Susannah married John Miller whose parents had emigrated to Rutherford County from North Ireland in the 1760s. Susannah and John built a farm on land provided by John's father and records show that they had a son, William Miller, who lived to the age of twelve and possibly two other children who lived to adulthood, John Twitty Miller and Susanna Lowry. John Miller represented Rutherford County in the NC legislature from 1801-1804. He died while attending court in Asheville in 1807. Susannah died in 1825.

Susannah is remembered as a patriot for her aid in repulsing the Tories from Graham's Fort in 1780. She is recognized by both the National Society Daughters of the American Revolution and the National Society Sons of the American Revolution. Susannah Twitty Miller, John Miller, and son William Miller are buried in the Miller-Twitty Cemetery on Mountain Creek in Rutherford County, North Carolina. Susannah Miller's flax spinning wheel remains in the possession of her descendants.

"Susannah
Wife of John Miller,
Died
April 14, 1825.
Age 62y 1 mo"

Susannah Miller, her husband John Miller, and their son William Miller are all buried outside of the iron fence at the Twitty-Miller Cemetery in Rutherford County.

Mary Hooks Slocumb

Mary "Polly" Hooks Slocumb (1760-1836), the daughter of Thomas Hooks and Anna Belotte, was born in Bertie County, North Carolina. She married Ezekial Slocumb, a resident of Wayne County, North Carolina, who would attain the rank of Colonel during the American Revolution. The Slocombs lived at Pleasant Green Plantation in Wayne County.

British Colonel Banastre Tarleton, in March 1781, headquartered at Pleasant Green and his cavalry numbering 1,000-1,100 encamped along the southern end of her property. At the time the house was occupied by Mary Slocumb, her sister, her child, and house servants. The plantation of the Slocumbs had been given the name "Pleasant Green" by Lord Cornwallis for its verdant green fields, and the name stuck. The events surrounding the occupation by Tarleton and his men are well-documented, having been penned by a friend of Mary Slocumb's as she dictated it.

One evening, a dinner served to Colonel Tarleton and his officers was followed by a particularly fine whiskey. The whiskey served by Mrs. Slocumb was praised by a Scottish officer who declared that he had never drunk any whiskey as good outside of Scotland. When he commented that the whiskey tasted like the smell of her orchard, Tarleton inquired where the spirits were procured. Mrs. Slocumb replied, "from the orchard where your tents stand." When conversation ensued concerning how the conquered lands would be divided among them, Tarleton replied that his officers would "receive large possession of the conquered American provinces," whereupon Mary Slocumb snapped, "Allow me to observe and prophesy, the only land in these United States which will ever remain in possession of a British officer, will measure but six feet by two!"

Lieutenant Slocumb at this time was scouting in the area two to three miles away, unknown to Banastre Tarleton and his men. When shots were fired nearby, Tarleton demanded that Mrs. Slocumb tell him whether Colonel Washington's troops were in the area. Mary Slocumb, fearing for the safety of her husband whom she knew to be nearby, replied, "I presume it is known to you that the Marquis [Lafayette] and [General Nathanael] Greene are in this state. And you would not of course be surprised at a call from Lee, or your old friend Colonel Washington, who, although a perfect gentleman, it is said shook your hand [pointing to the scar left by Washington's sabre] very rudely, when you last met." Mary Slocumb's reference was to the Battle of Cowpens in January 1781 in which Colonel William Washington struck Tarleton across the hand with his saber. In response, Tarleton had shot Washington's horse out from under him and fled the field after a disastrous defeat at the hands of the patriots and their commander General Daniel Morgan. In response, to Mary Slocumb's taunt, Tarleton called for his horse and disappeared through a break in the hedge to investigate the danger of her words.

With horror, Mary Slocumb spied her husband, her brother, and two of her neighbors galloping up the avenue of the plantation in pursuit of a Tory captain and four of his men who had been routed by Ezekial Slocumb. Lieutenant Slocumb unknowingly approached the encamped army of Colonel Tarleton whose tents were hidden from view by a hedgerow along the southern end of the property. Seeing a disaster at hand, a Slocumb slave named "Big George" jumped into their path along the avenue, shouted for Lieutenant Slocumb and pointed frantically to the left at the 1,000 men who were within firing range of Slocumb's small party of men. Without a pause, Slocumb and his men galloped directly towards the house where a Tory guard awaited them. When they reached the garden fence they jumped that one and the next, riding low to avoid a volley of gunfire, cleared the canal with one stupendous leap, and swept across the open field to the northwest where they were sheltered by woods before their pursuers could follow. The platoon that had been called out to pursue Slocumb was immediately recalled when Tarleton realized with dismay that Lieutenant Slocumb's party might be a scouting party to the larger contingent of Colonel Washington and Marquis de Lafayette's nearby army. Mary Slocumb's taunts had proven effective in saving the life of her husband and discouraging further pursuit by Tarleton.

When Tarleton returned to the house, he replied to Mary Slocumb, " Your husband made us a short visit, madam. I should have been happy to make his acquaintance, and that of his friend, Mr. Williams." Mary Slocumb responded caustically, "I have little doubt that you will meet the gentlemen, and they will thank you for the polite manner in which you treat their friends." Colonel Tarleton and his men took their dinner at the plantation and retired for the night with peach brandy unaware of any further activity taking place under cover of darkness.

Meanwhile, Lieutenant Slocumb and his men quietly circled the plantation, returning to the scene of the earlier encounter, and collected those men who had been separated from them. Near their encampment, Slocumb spotted a Tory who had been captured by patriots hanging from a tree with a bridle rein wrapped around his neck slowly choking him to death. Still kicking and struggling, Lieutenant Slocumb cut him down and spared his life.

Lieutenant Ezekial Slocumb and Major Williams raised an army of two hundred men from the surrounding countryside and continued to provoke Tarleton's army until Slocumb and Williams had crossed the Roanoke River where they joined Lafayette's army at Warrenton, North Carolina, where they would remain until the surrender at Yorktown.

When Colonel Tarleton and his army broke up their encampment at Pleasant Green Plantation, a sergeant was ordered by Colonel Tarleton to stand guard until the last soldier had departed to ensure the protection of Mary Slocumb who had impressed even him with her courage and decency.

But Mary Slocumb's most famous role in the Revolution was yet to come. It occurred at the Battle of Moore's Creek, one of the bloodiest battles of the Revolution and the first to take place in North Carolina. Royal Governor Josiah Martin called for troops to be raised in North Carolina in hopes of restoring the authority of the Crown in the colony. In answer, 1,600 Highland Scots and Loyalists gathered at Cross Creek (present-day Fayetteville) in a planned march to Wilmington under the command of General Donald McDonald.

In response, patriot Colonel James Moore devised a plan to cut off the rendezvous of Highland Scots with British regulars. He ordered Colonel Richard Caswell, a future governor of North Carolina, to march to Moore's Creek, near present day Wilmington. His troops were joined by those of Colonel Alexander Lillington, and their combined forces numbered 1,000 patriots. Together, Caswell and Lillington determined that Moore's Creek Bridge would serve as an excellent position of defense because the narrow bridge was situated at the highest elevation in the area, above a sandbar surrounded by swampy waters. The planks of the bridge were removed by the patriots, and the girders that supported them were generously greased. Caswell and Lillington divided their men and stationed them on either side of the river to wait.

General Donald McDonald, in the meantime, had fallen ill and turned over his command to Highlander Lieutenant Colonel Donald McLeod. McLeod led 1,500 men through chilly swamp waters in the dark of night as they stumbled around in the undergrowth. Eventually, they spied the abandoned camp of Caswell, who had left the embers of his campfires burning to confuse the enemy.

The Highlanders waited until dawn to attack the bridge. With broadswords in hand, and bagpipes skirling, the Highlanders raced for the bridge shouting, "King George and broadswords!" Those who made it onto the slippery bridge were swiftly cut down by patriot fire, and the battle was over within three minutes. Seventy Highlanders were killed including Lieutenant McLeod, and 850 were taken prisoner including the ailing General McDonald who was captured in his tent. Only one Whig, named John Grady, was killed.

Mary Slocumb experienced a vision of the battle as she related in her dictated notes: "As I lay whether waking or sleeping I know not I had a dream; yet it was not all a dream…I saw distinctly a body wrapped in my husband's guard-cloak bloody dead; and others dead and wounded on the ground about him. I saw them plainly and distinctly. I uttered a cry, and sprang to my feet on the floor: and so strong was the impression on my mind, that I rushed in the direction the vision appeared, and came up against the side of the house. The fire in the room gave little light, and I gazed in every direction to catch another glimpse of the scene. I raised the light; everything was still and quiet. My child was sleeping, but my woman was awakened by my crying out or jumping on the floor. If ever I felt fear it was at that moment. Seated on the bed, I reflected a few moments and said aloud: ' I must go to him.' I told the woman I could not sleep and would ride down the road. She appeared in great alarm; but I merely told her to lock the door after me, and look after the child. I went to the stable, saddled my mare as fleet and easy a nag as ever travelled; and in one minute we were tearing down the road at full speed."

Mary Slocumb galloped along the trail left by the troops. She encountered women and children fearfully standing in groups along the road waiting for news of their loved ones. At dawn, she heard the thundering sound of cannon fire as she approached the scene of the battle. She followed the Wilmington Road leading to Moore's Creek Bridge. Arriving at the scene of the battle, she spied twenty men lying wounded under the trees a few hundred yards below the bridge.

And then she saw her husband: "I saw all at once; but in an instant my whole soul was centered in one spot; for there, wrapped in his bloody guard cloak, was my husband's body! How I passed the few yards from my saddle to the place I never knew. I remember uncovering his head and seeing a face clothed with gore from a dreadful wound across the temple. I put my hand on the bloody face; 'twas warm; and an unknown voice begged for water. A small camp-kettle was lying near, and a stream of water was close by. I brought it; poured some in his mouth; washed his face; and behold it was Frank Cogdell. He soon revived and could speak. I was washing the wound in his head. Said he, ' It is not that; it is that hole in my leg that is killing me… Just then I looked up, and my husband, as bloody as a butcher, and as muddy as a ditcher, stood before me. 'Why, Mary!' he exclaimed, 'What are you doing there?'"

Mary Slocumb's legendary ride is said to have covered 65 miles, after which she tended to the wounded and dying at Moore's Creek Bridge. A monument to Mary Slocumb stands at the site of the Battle of Moore's Creek Bridge, Moore's Creek National Battlefield, in Currie, North Carolina. A statue of Mary rests on the top of the monument with the following inscriptions beneath on all four sides, one of the inscriptions memorializing the brave women of the lower Cape Fear region during the American Revolution:

"To The Honored Memory Of The Heroic Women Of The Lower Cape Fear During The American Revolution 1775-1781."

"Most Honored Of The Names Recorded By This Historic Association, Is That Of Mary Slocumb, Wife Of Lieutenant Slocumb, Riding Alone At Night 65 Miles To Succor The Wounded On This Battlefield. Her Heroism And Self-Sacrifice Place Her High On The Pages Of History And Should Awaken In Successive Generations, True Patriotism And Love Of Country. Virtutes Majorum Filiae Conservant"

"Unswerving In Devotion, Self-Sacrificing In Loyalty To The Cause Of Their Country, Their Works Do Follow Them; And Their Children Rise Up And Call Them Blessed."

"This Monument Was Erected By The Moore's Creek Monumental Association In The Year 1907."

Mary Slocumb is remembered as an American patriot for her role in defying the enemy and giving aid to her fallen countrymen. She is honored by both the National Society Daughters of the American Revolution and the National Society Sons of the American Revolution.

Mary Slocumb and her husband Ezekial Slocumb survived their turbulent role in the American Revolution. Their bodies were reinterred and now rest beneath the monument at Moore's Creek Bridge Battlefield. Their daughter, Susan Slocumb Graddy rests in the Nixon and Graddy Cemetery in Linden, Cumberland County, North Carolina.

The memorial to Mary Slocumb at Moore's Creek Bridge Battlefield with the graves of Ezekiel and Mary Slocumb in front.

Statue of Mary Slocumb at Moore's Creek Bridge Battlefield.

Elizabeth Maxwell Steele

An engraving of Elizabeth Maxwell Steele and General
Nathanael Greene by J.B. Hall. National Archives.

Elizabeth Maxwell (1733-1791) was born in Salisbury, Rowan County, in North Carolina. Her family was of Scots-Irish origin and emigrated from Pennsylvania to western North Carolina in 1733. Little is known of her early life, but it is known that her first husband was named Robert Gillespie and that he was scalped in 1760 by the Cherokee at Fort Dobbs in present day Iredell County during the French and Indian War. Their daughter, Margaret Gillespie married the Reverend Samuel Eusebius McCorkle, a Presbyterian minister who was pastor at Thyatira Presbyterian Church, established in 1749, and which still exists on Route 50 between Mooresville and Salisbury.

After the death of her first husband, Elizabeth married a man by the name of William Steele who died fourteen years later in 1774. Elizabeth Maxwell Steele and William Steele had a son by the name of John Steele. Elizabeth was forty years old at the time of William Steele's death. She was an ardent patriot and a skilled innkeeper who had managed to build a modest estate for herself and her son through land speculation and prudent management. Letters sent to her brother, Ephraim Steele in Carlisle, Pennsylvania, relate the depth of her patriotism as well as confirmations of her sterling character given by her descendants and contemporaries. The general consensus is that Elizabeth Maxwell Steele was a woman of steadfast determination and strength of will.

The Battle of Cowpens was fought in January 1781 with a decisive victory for the patriot forces over those of the British commanded by Colonel Banastre Tarleton. Known for his brutality and despised by the patriots, Tarleton had slaughtered the patriots after his victory at the Battle of the Waxhaws only eight months earlier. Patriot forces under Abraham Buford initially refused a command to surrender their forces though they eventually capitulated. In the meantime, Tarleton was shot at twice during the truce and his wounded horse fell on him, trapping him beneath. Infuriated, Tarleton ordered that no quarter be given to the disarmed patriots, and the British proceeded to slaughter them. Used as propaganda by the Continental Army, the legend of the brutality at the Waxhaws served to unite and rally the war effort, though men on both sides of the battle later questioned the truth of Tarleton's reputed retaliation. A young Andrew Jackson, a resident of the Waxhaws, would never forget the aftermath of the battle that day, and it served to stir up deep anti-British sentiment in him and many others.

General Daniel Morgan commanded the patriot forces at the Battle of Cowpens against Colonel Banastre Tarleton. A masterful bit of strategy by Morgan, postulated by some to be the most brilliant strategic move of the American Revolution, involved a double envelopment of the British forces by the patriots. As a result, Tarleton lost an estimated eighty-six percent of his fighting force in a crushing and humiliating defeat. The Battle of Cowpens (1781) together with the Battle of Kings Mountain three months prior (1780) succeeded in breaking British forces in the southern colonies and driving them northward to eventual defeat at Yorktown.

After Cowpens, Lord Cornwallis rapidly marched through the Carolinas, doggedly pursuing General Nathanael Greene's army, intent upon destroying them. Opposing Cornwallis' entry into North Carolina was General William Davidson who was killed at the Battle of Cowan's Ford one month after Cowpens, in Mecklenburg County, North Carolina, while trying to rally his men.

General Nathanael Greene, greatly disheartened at news of the death of Davidson, exhausted from evading Cornwallis and soaked from steady rains throughout the day, sought refuge at the inn of Elizabeth Maxwell Steele. A doctor by the name of Reed, charged with caring for wounded soldiers, took note of the dispirited General as he came through the door of the inn, and commented upon his appearance. "Yes," came the General's reply, "fatigued, hungry, alone and penniless!" He sat down at the table prepared to take a meal, when Mrs. Steele, who had overheard his cry of dejection quietly entered the room and shut the door behind her. She reminded the General of his despondent words and declared that she had overheard them. She reached down and withdrew two bags of money from her skirts and presented them to the General. "Take these, for you will want them and I can do without them," she said simply. Her generous gift, her words of encouragement, and her devotion to the cause greatly lifted General Greene's heart. He did not remain long at the inn, but before he left, he withdrew a portrait of King George which hung on the wall, and wrote on the back of it in chalk, "O George, hide thy face and mourn." He replaced the portrait with its face to the wall, and stepped out into the night to reunite with his troops.

Elizabeth Maxwell Steele is remembered as a patriot for her financial contribution to the cause of American independence by both the National Society

Daughters of the American Revolution and the National Society Sons of the American Revolution. She is probably more fondly remembered for her words of comfort to a despairing general. Elizabeth Maxwell Steele is buried in Thyatira Presbyterian Church, where her son-in-law the Reverend Samuel Eusebius McCorkle served as pastor.

Elizabeth Maxwell Steele's son, John Steele, became a member of the North Carolina State Legislature from 1789-1793. Presidents John Adams and Thomas Jefferson both appointed him as the Comptroller of the Treasury of North Carolina. John Steele's correspondence is housed at the University of North Carolina at Chapel Hill.

"Elizabeth Maxwell Steele
1733-1790
Salisbury - Feb. 1, 1781.

To Nathaniel Greene in the darkest hour of his career, she gave two bags of gold and silver saying: "Take these, General, you need them and I can do without them."

"This, that this woman hath done,
shall always be told as a memorial of her."

Oct. 7, 1948. Erected by the Elizabeth Maxwell Steele Chapter DAR, Salisbury, N.C., descendants and other patriotic citizens.

Kerenhappuch Norman Turner

Kerenhappuch Norman (1715-1781) is believed to have been born in Spotsylvania County, Virginia, to Isaac Norman (Jr.) and Frances Courtney Norman. Her father was a prominent planter, and Kerenhappuch married the son of a prominent tobacco planter, James Turner, in 1733. After their marriage, the Normans gifted James and Kerenhappuch Turner with 100 acres of the family plantation which lay on the Rappahannock River near present-day Remington, Virginia.

The Turners had five children: James (Jr.), Sarah, Mary, Elizabeth and Susan. The father and son were successful tobacco planters for many years. The land which they farmed was surveyed by a young George Washington in 1749 and was subsequently redrawn as Culpeper County. During this period, the Turner family became close friends with George Washington.

James and Kerenhappuch Turner sold their home and land in 1765 and moved to Halifax County, Virginia, though some accounts place their home in Maryland. James Turner (Sr.) died in 1773, but Kerenhappuch remained there and the American Revolution broke out in 1776. James Turner (Jr.) became a captain in the Virginia Militia. Kerenhappuch Turner, an accomplished horsewoman and a devoted patriot, delivered dispatches to the Continental army, even passing across enemy lines to do so.

The Battle of Guilford Court House took place in March 1781 in Guilford County, North Carolina. General Charles Cornwallis, with a force of fewer than 2,000 men defeated a much larger patriot force of between 4,000-5,000 men under the command of General Nathanael Greene. Though victorious, Cornwallis suffered heavy losses, possibly as much as one-fourth to one-third of his army, and so the Battle of Guilford Courthouse was viewed as a pyrrhic victory for the British, providing a strategic victory for the patriots.

Believing North Carolina to be fertile ground for Loyalist recruitment, Cornwallis had sought to enlist the aid of men loyal to the crown in hopes of reclaiming North Carolina for the British. A surprise defeat of the British at the Battle of Kings Mountain, followed by a strategic defeat at the Battle of Guilford Courthouse rapidly eroded British power in North Carolina, and Cornwallis was forced to abandon North Carolina altogether.

Eight members of Kerenhappuch Turner's family fought in the Battle of Guilford Courthouse, her son and seven grandsons. James Turner (Jr.) was seriously wounded, and when she learned about his injury she rode from her home in Virginia to the battlefield in North Carolina to tend to him. Upon her arrival, she moved her son to a log cabin on the battlefield and placed him in a makeshift bed on the floor. She then suspended tubs from the rafters after having bored holes in the tubs. Water from the nearby "Bloody Run" was used to fill the tubs which dripped water constantly down on her son's wounds and lowered his fever. James Turner (Jr.) survived because of his mother's devotion and quick thinking. Kerenhappuch nursed other wounded patriots from the Battle of Guilford Courthouse.

When the Revolution was over, Kerenhappuch Turner moved with her son and daughter, James (Jr.) and Sarah Turner, to Richmond County, North Carolina, where they lived on the Little River. Kerenhappuch remained an accomplished horsewoman and continued to ride and hunt with her family. In 1781, during one of those hunts, she was thrown from her horse and died from a broken neck.

The following is an excerpt from the address given at the unveiling of the Kerenhappuch Turner monument at the Guilford Court House Military Park on July 4, 1902:

"It is for me to tell you something of the brave woman in honor of whose memory we today unveil on this sacred spot the first monument ever erected on American soil to a Revolutionary heroine – its granite crowned with a handsome statue, and emblazoned with words of everlasting bronze. In song and in story – 'in thoughts that breathe and in words that burn' – have been told again and again the story of the virtues, the brave deeds, the sacrifice, the suffering, and the heroism of the men who fought, bled, and died in that terrible war for Independence; but the story of the privation, the suffering, the daring, and the dying of the grand reserve army of that war is yet untold and unsung.

"The women, by their lonely hearthstones, surrounded by helpless children, in the primeval forests, without mail or telegraph or railroad to bring them tidings of the absent loved ones their griefs, their sorrow, their suspense, their anxiety, their agony their death borne without a murmur. They died not in the exciting and exulting rush of battle. Theirs was the long slow, wasting, lingering death – a thousand deaths. Sometimes it was cold-blooded murder; sometimes it was the cold, piercing, cutting dagger of helpless grief; and sometimes they fell under the crushing burden of domestic care and trouble.

"Their battles were fought in the darkness and loneliness and silence of their homes. They heard not the martial music which thrilled heroes; they felt not the elbow touch which heroes feel in the mad rush of battle. There was never a shout or cheer to give them courage and strength. There were no medals awarded to them; no promotions were bestowed to stimulate them. Theirs was a lonely march to death – and yet how bravely and how patiently they fought to the end no tongue or pen can ever tell.

"These were heroines – and whilst in village, hamlet, town, and city, from ocean to ocean, we have with stone and brass built memorials of every name, size, and kind in honor of our heroes – the mothers, the wives, and the daughters of that awful time, who toiled and suffered and died for their country, are 'unwept, unhonored, and unsung.'

"Not only did they suffer and fight and toil thus in their lonely and desolate homes, but these ministers of compassion, these angels of pity, whenever possible, went to the battlefields to moisten the parched tongues, to bind the ghastly wounds, and to soothe the parting agonies alike of friend and foe, and to catch the last whispered messages of love from dying lips…"

Kerenhappuch Norman Turner's memorial stands at Guilford Courthouse National Military Park in Greensboro, Guilford County, North Carolina. She is remembered as a patriot for furnishing material aid to the cause of American independence by both the National Society Daughters of the American Revolution and the National Society Sons of the American Revolution.

Memorial to Kerenhappuch Norman Turner
Guilford Courthouse National Military Park
Greensboro, North Carolina.

Bibliography

Barefoot, Daniel W. *Touring North Carolina's Revolutionary War Sites*. Winston-Salem, N.C.: John F. Blair, Publisher, 1998.

Bulletin of the Genealogical Society of Old Tryon County. February 1990.

Dictionary of North Carolina Biography, 6 vols. Chapel Hill, N.C.: University of North Carolina Press, 1979-1996.

Dictionary of Virginia Biography, 3 vols. Richmond, VA.: Library of Virginia. 1998-2006.

Draper, Lyman C., *King's Mountain and Its Heroes: History of the Battle of King's Mountain and the Events Which Led to It*. Cincinnati: Peter G. Thomson, Publisher, 1881.

Ellet, Elizabeth F. *The Women of the American Revolution*. Vols. 1 and 2. Philadelphia: G.W. Jacobs & Co., 1900.

Griffin, Clarence W. *History of Old Tryon and Rutherford Counties, North Carolina, 1730-1936*. Asheville, N.C.: Miller Printing Co., 1937.

Kent, Scotti. *More Than Petticoats: Remarkable North Carolina Women*. Helena, MT: Falcon Publishing, Inc., 2000.

Kickler, Troy L. "Edenton Tea Party: An American First." *North Carolina History Project*. John Locke Foundation. Accessed March 21, 2017: www.northcarolinahistory.org/commentary/20/entry.

Kierner, Cynthia A. *Beyond the Household: Women's Place in the Early South, 1700-1835*. Comstock Classic Handbooks. Ithaca: Cornell University Press, 1998.

North Carolina Daughters of the American Revolution. *Roster of Soldiers from North Carolina in the American Revolution*. Reprint. Baltimore: Genealogical Publishing Co., 1984.

Phifer, Edward W. *Burke, the History of a North Carolina County, 1777-1920, with a Glimpse Beyond*. EW Phifer, 1982.

Rockbridge County, Virginia Heritage Book, 1778-1997. Rockbridge Baths, VA: Rockbridge Area Genealogical Society, 1997.

Rogers, Lou. *Tar Heel Women*. Raleigh, N.C.: Warren Publishing Co., 1949.

Samuel, Bill. *Quakerism in the 18th Century*. Originally published July 1, 1999 at Suite101.com. Accessed on: April 18, 2017: www.quakerinfo.com/quak_18.shtml.

Stewart, Mrs. W. S., II. *Markers Placed by the North Carolina Daughters of the American Revolution, 1900-1940*. Raleigh, N.C.: Edwards and Broughton, 1940.

The Colonial Records Project. Vol. 68, 214-236. Women Artisans in Backcountry North Carolina, 1753-1790. Johanna Miller Lewis. Jan-Michael Poff, Editor. Historical Publications Section. Raleigh, N.C. 1991. Accessed March 21, 2017: www.ncpublications.com/colonial/Nchr/Subjects/lewis.htm.

The Colonial Records Project. Vol. 58, 1-22. Women in Colonial North Carolina: Overlooked and Underestimated. Alan D. Watson. Jan-Michael Poff, Editor. Historical Publications Section. Raleigh, N.C. 1981. Accessed March 21, 2017: www.ncpublications.com/colonial/Nchr/Subjects/watson3.htm.

Williams, Claire R. (2014). *More Than a Housewife: Revolutionary Women in War*. In *JMU Scholarly Commons*. Paper presented at the Proceedings of the Fifth Annual Mad-Rush Undergraduate Research Conference: James Madison University.

Women of America. The American History and Genealogy Project. Wilmington, DE: The Perry-Nalle Publishing Co. ©August 2011-2017.

Photographic Credits

Armantia. "Gravestone for Grace Greenlee McDowell (1750-1823) Memorial No. 19036309." *Find a Grave*. Photograph accessed on March 20, 2017: www.findagrave.com/cgi-bin/fg.cgi?page=gr&GRid=20894216.

Bellard, Jan. "Gravestone for Rachel Craighead Caldwell (1739-1835) Memorial No. 47390146." *Find A Grave*. Photograph accessed on March 20, 2017: www.findagrave.com/cgi-bin/fg.cgi?page=gr&GRid=40478834.

Bobo, Ray. "Nancy Hart Highway Marker, Georgia Daughters of the American Revolution (1928); Nancy Hart Cabin (Replica) Marker, National Society Daughters of the American Revolution; Georgia Historical Commission Highway Marker (1955). Memorial No. 46978725." *Find A Grave*. Photograph accessed on March 28, 2017: www.findagrave.com/cgi-bin/fg.cgi?page=pv&GRid=16616031&PIpi=30220669.

Corrales-Diaz, Erin R. "Moore's Creek Women's Monument." *Commemorative Landscapes*. Photograph accessed on March 21, 2017: docsouth.unc.edu/commland/monument/305. www.findagrave.com/cgi-bin/fg.cgi?page=cr&GRid=2180&CRid=16162&.

Dawes, Philip. "A Society of Patriotic Ladies, at Edenton in North Carolina." Mezzotint. London, March 25, 1775. North Carolina Office of Archives and History, Raleigh, NC.

Franklin, Denise R. "Gravestone for Sarah Robinson Erwin (1750-1785) Memorial No. 46877556." *Find A Grave*. Photograph accessed on March 19, 2017: www.findagrave.com/cgi-bin/fg.cgi?page=gr&GRid=19428738.

Grant, Michele Lee. "A Statue of Mary Slocumb at Moore's Creek Battlefield." ©2008. Photograph accessed on March 21, 2017: www.learnnc.org/lp/multimedia/10355.

Hagerman, Polly Fry. "Gravestone for Martha MacFarlane Bell (1735-1820) Memorial No. 47161889." *Find A Grave*. Photograph accessed on March 20, 2017: www.findagrave.com/cgi-bin/fg.cgi?page=gr&GRid=17972512.

Hartge, John. "Gravestone for Margaret Sharpe Gaston (1755-1812). Memorial No. 47172774." *Find A Grave*. Photograph accessed on April 17, 2017: www.findagrave.com/cgi-in/fg.cgi?page=pv&GRid=93766882&PIpi=63700749.

Hepler, Jim. "Buffalo Presbyterian Church Cemetery in Greensboro, Guilford County, North Carolina, Memorial No. 46977053." *Find A Grave*. Photograph accessed on March 20, 2017: www.findagrave.com/cgi-bin/fg.cgi?page=gr&GRid=40478834.

Jordan, Mark. "Gravestone for Nancy Morgan Hart (1735-1830) Memorial No. 46874400." *Find A Grave*. Photograph accessed on March 28, 2017: www.findagrave.com/cgi-bin/fg.cgi?page=pv&GRid=16616031&PIpi=4536101.

McGee, Heather. "Gravestone for Martha MacFarlane Bell (1735-1820) Memorial No. 46926529." *Find A Grave*. Photograph accessed on March 20, 2017: www.findagrave.com/cgi-bin/fg.cgi?page=gr&GRid=17972512.

Miller, Kelly. "Gravestone for Elizabeth Maxwell Steel (1733-1790) Memorial No. 22404613." *Find A Grave*. Photograph accessed on March 21, 2017: www.findagrave.com/cgi-bin/fg.cgi?page=gr&GRid=22404613.

Mills, Kathy. "Gravestone for Hannah Millikan Blair (1756-1852) Memorial No. 46610041." *Find A Grave*. Photograph accessed on April 17, 2017: www.findagrave.com/cgi-in/fg.cgi?page=pv&GRid=16032706&PIpi=10119441.

"Mrs. Penelope Barker/President of the Edenton Tea Party of 1774." Image. North Carolina Museum of History, Raleigh, NC.

Perrys. "Gravestone for Penelope Padgett Barker (1728-1796) Memorial No. 46849660." *Find A Grave*. Photograph accessed on March 20, 2017: www.findagrave.com/cgi-bin/fg.cgi?page=gr&GRid=33444070.

Reed, Elizabeth. "Gravestone for Mary Hooks Slocumb (1760-1836) Memorial No. 46561848." *Find A Grave*. Photograph accessed on March 21, 2017: www.findagrave.com/cgi-bin/fg.cgi?page=gr&GRid=21278323.

Streck, Chris. "Gravestone for Susanna Twitty Miller (1763-1825); "Photograph of Miller-Twitty Cemetery, Rutherford County, North Carolina. Memorial No. 48697907." *Find A Grave*. Photograph accessed on March 22, 2017: www.findagrave.com/cgi-bin/fg.cgi?page=gr&GRid=90326262.

Thomas, Donna. "Gravestone for Annie Edminsten McDowell (1730-1814) Memorial No. 47586188." *Find A Grave*. Photograph accessed on March 19, 2017: www.findagrave.com/cgi-bin/fg.cgi?page=gr&GRid=59651654.

-------, Pat. "Gravestone for Martha MacFarlane Bell (1735-1820) Memorial No. 47158120." *Find A Grave*. Photograph accessed on March 20, 2017: www.findagrave.com/cgi-bin/fg.cgi?page=gr&GRid=17972512.

-------, Sam. "Memorial Statue for Kerenhappuch Norman Turner at Guilford Courthouse National Military Park in Greensboro, Guilford County, North Carolina. Memorial No. 47263334." *Find A Grave*. Photograph accessed on March 22, 2017: www.findagrave.com/cgi-bin/fg.cgi?page=gr&GRid=43721050.

www.ingramcontent.com/pod-product-compliance
Lightning Source LLC
Chambersburg PA
CBHW081350040426
42450CB00015B/3387